BIG CATS

Carly Blake

WINDMILL
BOOKS ™

New York

Published in 2015 by Windmill Books, An Imprint of Rosen Publishing
29 East 21st Street, New York, NY 10010

US Editor: Joshua Shadowens
Publishing Director: Belinda Gallagher
Creative Director: Jo Cowan
Editorial Assistant: Carly Blake
Volume Design: Sally Lace
Cover Designer: Jo Cowan
Image Manager: Liberty Newton
Indexer: Hilary Bird
Production Manager: Elizabeth Collins
Reprographics: Stephan Davis, Thom Allaway, Lorraine King

All artwork from the Miles Kelly Artwork Bank
Cover niall dunne/Shutterstock.com
Fotolia 13 Judy Whitton
Shutterstock.com 3 Igor Zakowski; 7 Ilaszlo;
9 Chris Kruger; 15 Leksele; 18 Pal Teravagimov

All other photographs are from:
digitalSTOCK, digitalvision, John Foxx, PhotoAlto, PhotoDisc, PhotoEssentials, PhotoPro, Stockbyte

Library of Congress Cataloging-in-Publication Data

Blake, Carly, author.
 Big cats / by Carly Blake.
     pages cm. — (Animal Q & A)
 Includes index.
 ISBN 978-1-4777-9182-0 (library binding) — ISBN 978-1-4777-9183-7 (pbk.) —
ISBN 978-1-4777-9184-4 (6-pack)
 1. Felidae—Miscellanea—Juvenile literature. 2. Lion—Juvenile literature. 3. Tiger—Juvenile literature. 4. Children's questions and answers. I. Title.
 QL737.C23B58 2015
 599.75—dc23
                        2014001236

Contents

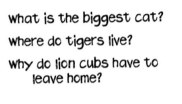

what is the biggest cat?

The Siberian tiger is the biggest cat, and one of the largest meat-eating animals in the world. The heaviest Siberian tiger was recorded at weighing 1,025 pounds (465 kg) – that's the same weight as 23 of you! It also has thick fur to help it survive in freezing conditions.

where do tigers live?

Tigers only live in southern and eastern Asia, in forests, woodlands and swamps. They used to live in much larger areas, but humans have now built houses and farms on much of the land. Siberian tigers live in snow-covered forests where temperatures can be -58°F (-50°C).

Siberian tiger

Hair-head!

Male lion cubs begin to grow thick fur around their head and neck at about three years old. This fur is called a mane.

why do lion cubs have to leave home?

Male lion cubs don't get to stay with their family group or pride. They get pushed out at about three years old. By then they are old enough to look after themselves. Soon they will take over new prides and have their own cubs.

Discover

Tigers are only found in certain parts of the world. Look on a map and see if you can find them.

Do big cats live in groups?

Lions are the only big cats that live in large family groups, called prides. A pride is normally made up of four to six female lions, one or two males and their cubs. Some prides may have up to 30 animals if there is plenty of food nearby.

Pride of lions

Pretend

Imagine you are a prowling lion creeping up on your prey. See how slowly and quietly you can move.

which cats can scream?

Small cats such as pumas make an ear-piercing scream instead of a roar. The cat family can be divided into two groups – big cats that can roar, and small cats that can't. A screaming cat can still be just as frightening!

why are lions lazy?

Lions seem lazy, but they have to rest to keep cool in the hot African sun. Usually, lions rest for around 20 hours a day. They normally hunt in the morning or at night when it's coolest. After a big meal they don't need to eat again for several days.

why are tigers stripy?

Tigers are stripy to help them blend into their shadowy, leafy surroundings. Stripes also help to hide the shape of the tiger's body, making hunting easier. White tigers born in the wild are less likely to live as long as orange tigers because they do not blend in as well.

Tiger cubs

Lynx

which cat is in danger?

Lynx numbers are falling because of the drop in the number of rabbits, which are their main food. The Iberian lynx, found in Spain and Portugal, is the most endangered cat. This is because humans have cut down many forests where they live.

what do ocelots eat?

Ocelots, also called painted leopards, are small wild cats found mainly in South and Central America. They eat lots of different foods including rats, birds, frogs, monkeys, fish, tortoises and deer.

Think

How many types of food do you eat in a day? Is it as many as an ocelot?

Going, gone!

It's too late for some big cats. The Taiwan clouded leopard, and the Caspian, Bali and Javan tigers are extinct (have died out).

what is the bounciest cat?

The bounciest cat is the African serval. It can leap 3 feet (1 m) high and travel 13 feet (4 m) as it jumps. Unusually, it hunts in the day, for frogs, locusts and voles. Servals are like cheetahs, with slim, graceful, spotty bodies.

Serval

Do cats change their coats?

The lynx changes its coat with the weather. It lives in forests in northern Europe and Asia. In summer, the lynx's coat is short and light brown, but in winter its coat is much thicker, and light gray. This helps it to hide throughout the year.

Paw prints!

The stripes on a tiger are a bit like our fingerprints – no two animals have exactly the same pattern on their coats.

Why does a lion roar?

Lions roar to scare off other lions that stray onto their patch of land or territory. They also roar to let other members of their pride know where they are. A lion's roar is so loud it can be heard up to 6 miles (10 km) away!

Roaring lion

Wear

Cats are kept warm by their thick coats of fur. Put on some furry clothes. Do they keep you warm?

why do leopards climb trees?

Leopards climb trees to rest or to eat their food in safety. These big cats often kill prey that is larger than themselves. They are excellent climbers and are strong enough to drag their prey up into a tree, away from other hungry animals.

Leopard

How can humans help big cats?

Humans can help big cats by protecting areas of rain forest and grassland where they live. These areas are called reserves. In a reserve, trees are not allowed to be cut down and the animals can live in safety.

Puma

No boat? Float!

Ancient Chinese soldiers used blown-up animal skins to cross deep rivers. They used their mouths to blow in air, then covered them with grease to keep it in.

What is a puma's favorite food?

Rabbits, hares and rats are favorite foods for a puma. They will attack bigger animals too. In places where humans have built their homes near the puma's natural surroundings, people have been attacked by these cats.

Can cheetahs run fast?

Yes they can – cheetahs are the world's fastest land animal. In a few seconds of starting a chase, a cheetah can reach its top speed of 65 miles per hour (105 km/h) – as fast as a car! Cheetahs have 30 seconds to catch their prey before they run out of energy.

Why do people hunt big cats?

Mainly for their beautiful fur. For many years, cats have been killed by the hundreds of thousands so that people can wear their skins. Tigers especially were hunted for their body parts, which were used in Chinese medicines.

Make
With a paper plate and some straws for whiskers, make a tiger mask. Cut out eyeholes and paint it stripy!

can't catch me!

Even though cheetahs are super-fast runners, only half of their chases end with a catch. Sometimes they scare their prey off before they get close enough to pounce.

Cheetah

Tiger

what time do tigers go hunting?

Almost all cats, including tigers, hunt at night. It is easier for a tiger to creep up on its prey when there is less light. A tiger may travel many miles (km) each night while hunting. Tigers hunt deer, wild pigs, cattle and monkeys.

15

where do cheetahs live?

Cheetahs live in grasslands called savannas. The savanna is dry, flat and open land, and is home to many other animals including gazelles, wildebeest and zebra. One of the best-known savannas is the Serengeti in Africa.

Cheetahs hunting in the savanna

why do cats wash their faces?

Cats wash their faces to spread their scent over their body. Cats have scent-producing body parts called glands on their chin. They use their paws to wipe the scent from their glands and when the cat walks, it can mark its area, or territory.

Lion

Play

With a friend, collect some pebbles and sticks and use them to mark out your own territories in your garden.

Slow down!

In the wild, cheetahs have a short lifespan. Their running speed gets a lot slower as they get older so they are less successful when they hunt.

How often do tigers eat?

Sometimes, tigers don't even eat once a week. When tigers catch an animal they can eat 80 pounds (40 kg) of meat. They don't need to eat again for eight or nine days.

what is a group of cubs called?

A group of cubs is called a litter. There are usually between two and four cubs in every litter. Cubs need their mother's milk for the first few months, but gradually they start to eat meat. The young of some cats, such as the puma, are called kittens.

Mother puma and litter of kittens

Sharpen your claws!

Unlike other cats, a cheetah's claws don't go back into its paws. This is why they don't often climb trees – they find it hard to get back down.

Leopards fighting

Why do leopards fight each other?

Leopards fight each other to defend their territory. Each leopard has its own patch of land, which it lives in. Leopards use scent-marking and make scratches on certain trees to warn other cats away.

Draw

Many different animals live in trees. Draw some pictures of animals that live in trees near you.

Which cat lives in the treetops?

Clouded leopards are excellent climbers and spend much of their time in the treetops of their forest home. These animals have been seen hanging upside-down from branches only by their back legs. Clouded leopards are brilliant swimmers, too.

which big cats live in rain forests?

Tigers and leopards live in rain forests in India, and jaguars live in South American rain forests. Here, the weather stays hot all year, although there is often lots of rain.

Jaguar

what animals do jaguars hunt?

Young jaguars climb trees to hunt for birds and small animals. Adults are too heavy for the branches and hunt on the ground for deer, small mammals and sometimes cattle and horses.

Think

Are you as playful as the lion cubs? Invent some new games of your own to play with your friends.

Lion cubs

How do cubs learn to hunt?

Cubs learn to hunt by playing. Even a tortoise is a fun toy and by playing like this, cubs learn hunting skills. Many mothers bring their cubs a small, live animal so they can practice catching it.

It's a wrap!

The ancient Egyptians are well known for their mummies. They even mummified animals including cats, birds and crocodiles.

why are cats the perfect hunters?

Because they have excellent eyesight and hearing, strong bodies and sharp teeth and claws. Many cats, such as lions, have fur that blends into their surroundings, which means they can hunt while staying hidden.

Lion hunting

Glossary

claws (KLAWZ) The sharp parts of an animal's feet.

endangered (in-DAYN-jerd) In danger of no longer existing.

life span (LYF SPAN) The amount of time that something is alive.

litter (LIH-ter) A group of kittens born to the same mother at the same time.

mane (MAYN) Long hair on the necks of certain animals.

prey (PRAY) An animal that is hunted by another animal for food.

pride (PRYD) A group of lions that live together.

rain forest (RAYN FOR-est) A thick forest that receives a large amount of rain during the year.

reserves (rih-ZURVZ) Land set aside for wildlife.

savanna (suh-VA-nuh) An area of grassland with few trees or bushes.

territory (TER-uh-tor-ee) Land or space that is protected by an animal for its use.

voles (VOHL) A mouse-like animal.

Further Reading

Gray, Peter. *How to Draw Tigers and Other Big Cats.* How to Draw Animals. New York: PowerKids Press, 2014.

Marzolf, Julie. *Big Cats Are Not Pets!* When Pets Attack! New York: Gareth Stevens Publishing, 2014.

Owen, Ruth. *Carnivorous Big Cats.* Eye to Eye with Animals. New York: Windmill Books, 2013.

Index

websites

For web resources related to the subject of this book, go to:
www.windmillbooks.com/weblinks and select this book's title.